D1613735

Life Under the Sea
Sharks

by Cari Meister

Bullfrog Books

Ideas for Parents and Teachers

Bullfrog Books let children practice reading informational text at the earliest reading levels. Repetition, familiar words, and photo labels support early readers.

Before Reading

- Ask the child to think about sharks. Ask: What do you know about sharks?
- Look at the picture glossary together. Read and discuss the words.

Read the Book

- Read the book to the child, or have him or her read independently.
- Point out the photo labels to reinforce new vocabulary as you read.

After Reading

- Prompt the child to think more. Ask: Which types of shark do you like the best? Why?

Bullfrog Books are published by Jump!
5357 Penn Avenue South
Minneapolis, MN 55419
www.jumplibrary.com

Library of Congress Cataloging-in-Publication Data
Meister, Cari.
   Sharks / by Cari Meister.
     p. cm. -- (Bullfrog books. Life under the sea)
   Summary: "This photo-illustrated book for early readers tells about many different kinds of sharks and the unique features of species like the Hammerhead and the Great White shark"-- Provided by publisher.
   Audience: K to grade 3.
   Includes bibliographical references and index.
   ISBN 978-1-62031-035-9 (hardcover : alk. paper) -- ISBN 978-1-62496-053-6 (ebook)
   1. Sharks--Juvenile literature. 2. Sharks--Behavior--Juvenile literature. I. Title.
QL638.9.M5227 2014
597.3--dc23   2013001961

Series Editor   Rebecca Glaser
Book Designer   Ellen Huber
Photo Researcher   Heather Dreisbach

Photo Credits: Alamy, 14, 15, 20, 21, 23tr; Dreamstime, cover, 7, 22; Getty, 5; National Geographic, 19; SeaPics, 12, 13; Shutterstock, 3, 4, 6, 8, 17, 23bl, 23br, 24; SuperStock, 1, 9, 10, 11, 18; Veer, 16, 23tl

Printed in the United States of America at Corporate Graphics, North Mankato, Minnesota.
5 2013 / PO 1003

10 9 8 7 6 5 4 3 2 1

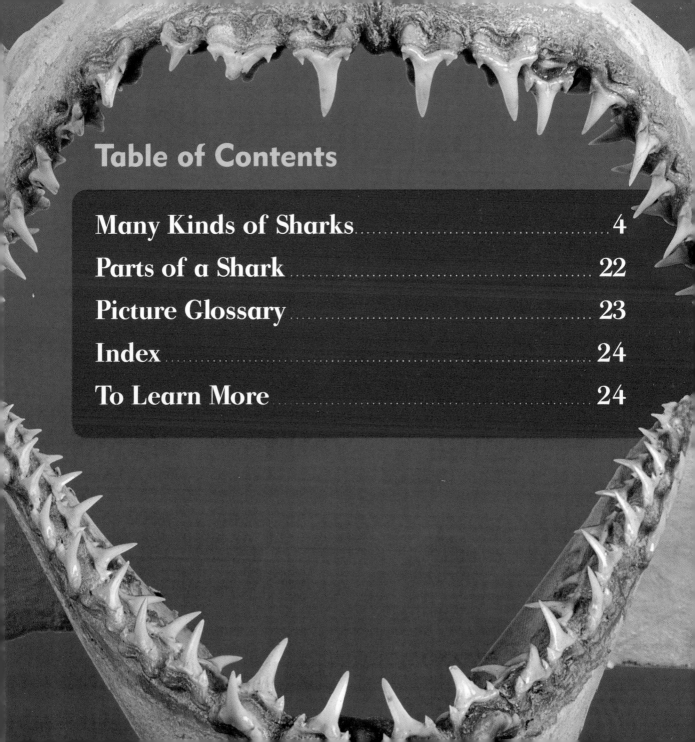

Table of Contents

Many Kinds of Sharks

Here comes a whale shark.
It's bigger than a bus!

Don't worry.
It won't eat you.
Whale sharks
eat plankton.

plankton

They eat small fish, too.

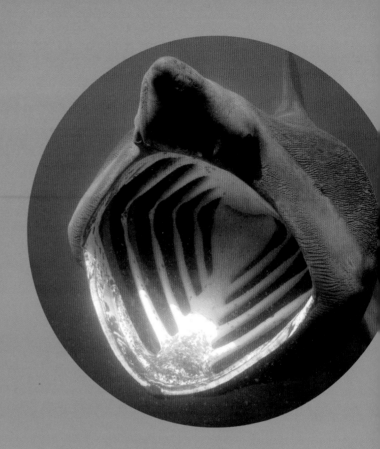

There are many
kinds of sharks.

Very few eat people.

This is a hammerhead.

Do you see
its eyes?

They can see
all around.

Look at this goblin shark.
He lives in the deep.

He has a long snout.
It helps find prey.

14

A mako is the fastest shark.

His body bends to swim fast.

15

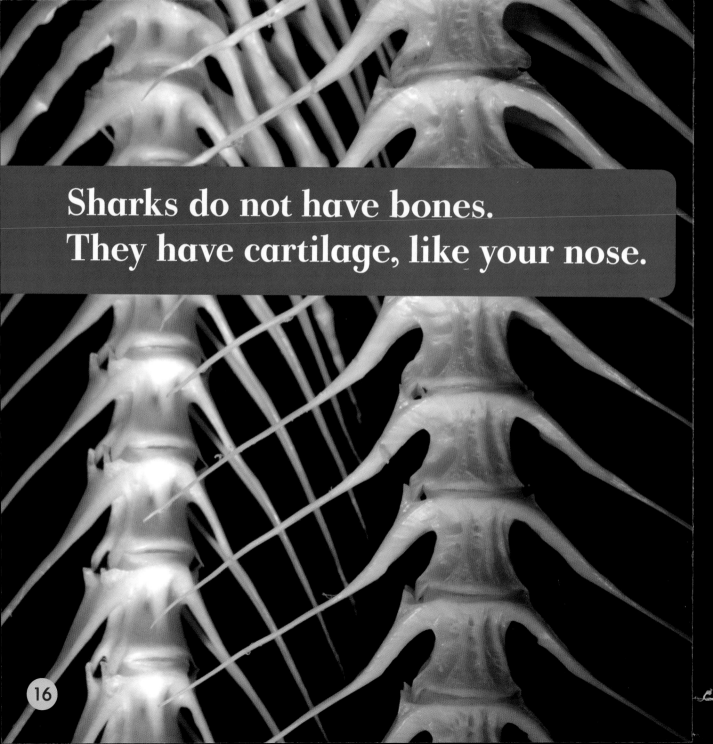

Sharks do not have bones.
They have cartilage, like your nose.

It is bendy.

nostril

A great white
shark hunts.

His nostrils smell.

His eyes look.

A sea lion! Yum!

Parts of a Shark

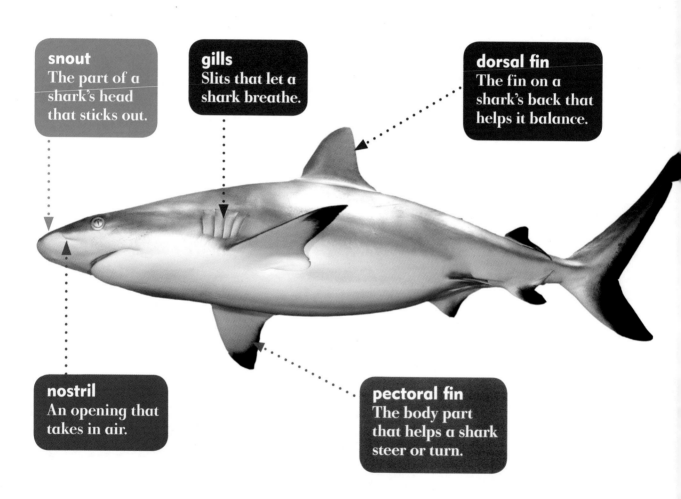

snout
The part of a shark's head that sticks out.

gills
Slits that let a shark breathe.

dorsal fin
The fin on a shark's back that helps it balance.

nostril
An opening that takes in air.

pectoral fin
The body part that helps a shark steer or turn.

Picture Glossary

cartilage
A strong, bendy type of tissue.

prey
An animal hunted for food.

plankton
Tiny animals that float in ocean water.

sea lion
A large animal that looks like a seal, with large flippers and ears that stick out.

Index

To Learn More

Learning more is as easy as 1, 2, 3.

1) Go to www.factsurfer.com

2) Enter "shark" into the search box.

3) Click the "Surf" button to see a list of websites.

With factsurfer.com, finding more information is just a click away.